P9-DNN-487

Uncle Jack Is a Carpenter

Written by Charnan Simon • Illustrated by Robert Squier

Published in the United States of America by The Child's World®
PO Box 326 • Chanhassen, MN 55317-0326
800-599-READ • www.childsworld.com

Reading Adviser

Cecilia Minden-Cupp, PhD, Former Language and Literacy Program Director,
Harvard Graduate School of Education, Cambridge, Massachusetts

Acknowledgments

The Child's World®: Mary Berendes, Publishing Director

Editorial Directions, Inc.: E. Russell Primm, Editorial Director and Project Manager;
Katie Marsico, Associate Editor; Judith Shiffer, Assistant Editor; Caroline Wood, Editorial Assistant

The Design Lab: Kathleen Petelinsek, Design and Art Production

Library of Congress Cataloging-in-Publication Data

Simon, Charnan.
  Uncle Jack is a carpenter / written by Charnan Simon; illustrated by Robert Squier.
    p. cm. —(Magic door to learning)
  ISBN 1-59296-618-7 (library bound : alk. paper)
  1. Carpentry—Juvenile literature. 2. Carpenters—Juvenile literature.
  I. Squier, Robert. II. Title. III. Series.
  TH5607.S56 2006
  694—dc22   2006001410

A book is a door, a magic door.
It can take you places
you have never been before.
Ready? Set?
Turn the page.
Open the door.
Now it is time to explore.

My Uncle Jack is a carpenter. He builds houses all over town. Today he has a special job—and I am his helper!

Uncle Jack rolls out his plans.
"This is a blueprint," he says.

"A blueprint shows us how
to put our project together." 7

We make a list.
We need wood and
nails and shingles.
We need hammers
and saws and paint.

We jump in Uncle Jack's van.
We roll down the windows
and sing as we drive.

The lumber yard is big
and busy. I help carry
our supplies. Carpenters
and their helpers need
to be strong!

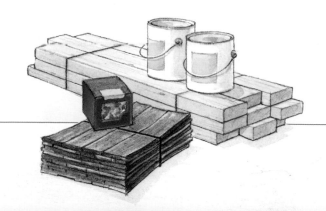

Next comes the roof.
"Raise the roof beams
high, carpenter!" Uncle
Jack sings out. I hand
him the shingles.

Bam! Bam! Bam!
Uncle Jack hammers away.
Up go the walls!
In go the windows!
In goes the door!

Painting is the fun part.
Swish! Swish!

I dip my paintbrush in the can—
and I don't spill much at all!

21

My Uncle Jack is a carpenter. He builds houses all over town. Today WE built a house together just for me!

Our story is over, but there is still much to explore beyond the magic door!

Did you know that you can build your own miniature house from a shoebox? With an adult's help, cut out two rectangles for a front door and a back door. Cut out squares for as many windows as you like. Use construction paper and markers to decorate the outside of your house. If you have time, draw the people who live inside your house along one of the sides of the shoebox.

These books will help you explore at the library and at home:

Johnson, D. B. *Henry Builds a Cabin.* Boston: Houghton Mifflin, 2002.
Sobel, June, and Melissa Iwai (illustrator). *B Is for Bulldozer: A Construction ABC.* San Diego: Harcourt, 2003.

About the Author

Charnan Simon lives in Madison, Wisconsin, where she can usually be found sitting at her desk and writing books, unless she is sitting at her desk and looking out the window. Charnan has one husband, two daughters, and two very helpful cats.

About the Illustrator

Robert Squier loves to illustrate stories using watercolor, ink, and colored pencil. When he's not drawing in Portsmouth, New Hampshire, you can find him ballroom dancing or camping.

Back at home, Uncle Jack
builds a frame. I help a little.